JOHN LAWRENCE

Lovable Loser

Copyright © 2024 by John Lawrence

All rights reserved. No part of this publication may be reproduced, stored or transmitted in any form or by any means, electronic, mechanical, photocopying, recording, scanning, or otherwise without written permission from the publisher. It is illegal to copy this book, post it to a website, or distribute it by any other means without permission.

John Lawrence asserts the moral right to be identified as the author of this work.

John Lawrence has no responsibility for the persistence or accuracy of URLs for external or third-party Internet Websites referred to in this publication and does not guarantee that any content on such Websites is, or will remain, accurate or appropriate.

Designations used by companies to distinguish their products are often claimed as trademarks. All brand names and product names used in this book and on its cover are trade names, service marks, trademarks and registered trademarks of their respective owners. The publishers and the book are not associated with any product or vendor mentioned in this book. None of the companies referenced within the book have endorsed the book.

First edition

*This book was professionally typeset on Reedsy.
Find out more at reedsy.com*

Contents

First Inning	1
Second Inning: Becoming a Cubs Fan	3
Third Inning: Firsts	7
Fourth Inning: Park District Mayhem	12
Fifth Inning: Grown Up Cubs Fan	17
Sixth Inning: Helping Your Kids Become Cubs Fans (OK...	24
Seventh Inning: 36 in a Row!	29
Eighth Inning: The Magic Year!	37
Ninth Inning: The Curse Breaker	42
Post Game Interview	45

First Inning

What is a baseballography?

This is a good question to ask, especially if you've never heard of a baseballography. Well, you probably have not heard of a baseballography since I made up the word when deciding to write this book.

A baseballography is a biography of a person who has loved baseball for most if not all of his life. It is kind of a love child of a baseball nut and an autobiography. They went on a first date to a baseball game, fell in love with baseball, and developed a story around it. Thus, you have a baseballography.

It's the Cubs, OK!

For those of you who are not fans of a professional baseball team on the northside of Chicago, this is a story of a Cubs fan. Except for the team, this could be the journey of any baseball fan over the years. I mean, it would be different if you cheered on a team that won a lot of World Series Championships, because I have no idea what a life like that is like.

Journey of Many Memories – Funny – Touching – Amazing – Shared – oh, and Ones Where You Lost . . . a lot!

Since this is a baseballography, it is going to be about the memories I have had as a lifelong Cubs fan. Many of them will be funny because of my personal history of watching the Cubs lose games live. Some will be touching, because I shared them with my dad and also as a dad. Some will be Amazing, with thrilling stories of watching victory crumble into defeat. Some will be shared by anyone who has loved baseball. Oh, and If I have not mentioned it already, there will be stories of losing . . . a lot. I do want to offer a teaser in this introduction for the readers. This is also about the end of an era (imagine that resounding like when Lou Gehrig made his "Luckiest Man" speech). Believe me, the end of this era was not as moving as that speech, but you can't fault me for trying.

Second Inning: Becoming a Cubs Fan

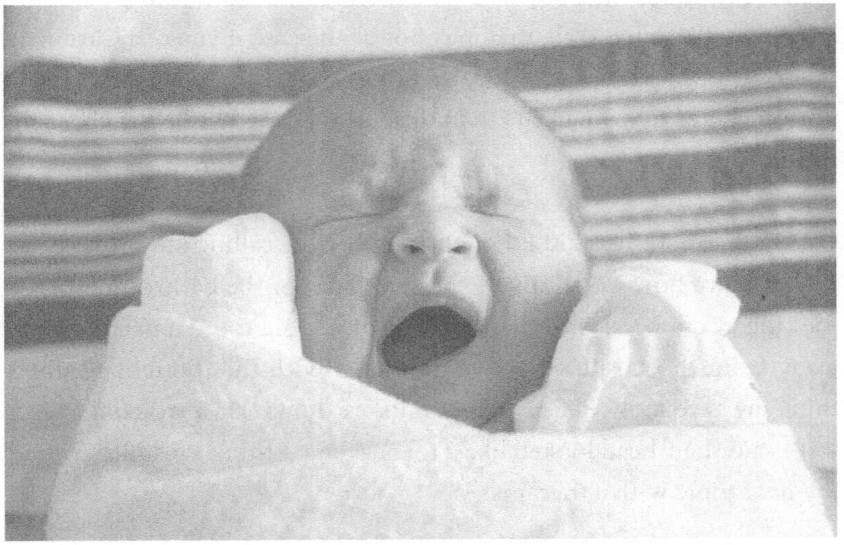

Be Born

The first thing you have to do to be a Cubs fan is that you have to be born. I mean, this is a baseballography, so at some point I had to have been born. I actually did a study (that I made up in my mind, but is totally fake) and found that 100% of all Cubs fans have been born at some point in their earliest days of life – usually at the beginning. So . . . I was born. Leroy and Marie had their third bouncing baby boy on May 30th in Joliet, Illinois. A Cubs fan was born!

Live in or Near Chicago

The second thing in order to be a Cubs fan is to live in or near Chicago. This is not a mandated item – but it sure helps. There is nothing cuter than a towheaded little boy with a Cubs shirt and one of those "made for a kid" baseball hats. Well, that may not be the case if you're a Cardinals fan – or a Mets fan – or a Pirates fan – or . . . well, maybe there is nothing cuter to my parents than their tow-headed little boy cheering for the Cubs.

On another note, as a kid I thought people were calling me a "toe" head. I'm not sure how much time I spent in front of the bathroom mirror looking at my head, and then looking at my big toe. I'd usually walk away from those self-reflective moments with the thought, "I don't think my head looks like my toe. Adults are dumb. How would they like it if I said their head looked like a toe!" Whoa – think I just discovered my next topic with a therapist.

Have a Big Brother Who is a White Sox Fan

I had a big brother. He was a White Sox fan. He was also one of the people who I enjoyed annoying more than anyone on earth. My mother would catch us in our latest arguments where he said, "Up," and I immediately responded with, "Down." She would roll her eyes – and desperately try to get dad into the room so that he could do his best Henry Kissinger impression and break up the fight. He wasn't a very good Kissinger, though. Well, unless Henry walked into negotiations

SECOND INNING: BECOMING A CUBS FAN

and smacked both parties I the back of the head and said, "Knock it off you knuckleheads!" Hmmm, bet that would work better than all that stuff they do at the U.N. But I digress (I'd get used to that if I were you).

He was a White Sox fan and that meant that I was predestined to be a Cubs fan. Since that annoyed him, I became a die-hard Cubs fan. A choice based on deep research, acute baseball acumen, and how red I could make him turn by driving him crazy.

Have a Park District that only Goes to Cubs Games

The next step to becoming a Cubs fan is to have a Park District that only goes to Cubs games. I played T-ball as a part of the Lockport Park District. It was there where I was assigned to be on the Pirates, ugh! But it was also there where I got to go to Cubs games once or twice a summer. For some reason they only went to Cubs games each year. So, the whole "predestined to be a Cubs fan" thing was confirmed again. Later on, this also was a source of annoyance to my older brother who got a summer job doing – you got it – T-ball with the Lockport Park District. Some things are just icing on the cake.

Be OK with Disappointment

This is an important step to being a Cubs fan. You have to be OK with your team losing. You also need to understand disappointment around playoff time. Shoot, there were years when disappointment came at the All-Star break.

Disappointment never made a true Cubs fan think about cheering for another team. Wait until next year was our mantra! Even as a kid I seemed to be OK with my team never winning the World Series. Cubs fans live with a sense of eternal hope, as well as looking for any way to be nice to a goat if they happen to show up anywhere near Wrigley Field.

One of the ways that I learned to deal with disappointment was in how the Cubs seemed to lose every time I showed up at a live game at Wrigley – or any other venue where they would play. There will be more about that in future innings.

Third Inning: Firsts

First Game – Park District Trip

A baseballography will be filled with "firsts." For me this brought back a flood of memories of firsts I had with the Cubs. The first of my firsts was going to my initial Cubs game at Wrigley in

Chicago. That was also my first outing with the Lockport Park District T-ball group! We'll have an entire inning devoted to those wonderful days.

First Time Wanting to Throw Up

Going to a Major League Baseball game also means being exposed to this amazing environment where people walk up and down the stands offering you hot dogs, drinks, peanuts, and a strange sticky substance called cotton candy. You didn't even have to go to a stand somewhere, they brought it right to you. This created true community as you passed your money through the hands of 10-15 other people and astoundingly – they would pass you back your food item along with your change!

It was also the first time I was at a public event and wanted to throw up. It seems that when you unleash a group of 6 to 8 year olds in an environment where they offer food throughout a nine-inning, 3 hour period, they will eat so much of it that they will want to barf. By the way, a mixture of Coca-cola, hot dogs, peanuts, and cotton candy is really gross – especially when it lands on your new Converse gym shoes. Oh, another thing – mom is not happy with your new Converse air-barfs when you get home.

First Time You KNOW You're Going to Catch a Foul Ball!

If you're a kid and a fan, and you go to a game, you're going to bring your baseball glove. Scratch that – you're going to wear your baseball glove. You will most likely put it on before you get on the bus, wear it all the way to Chicago, wear it for the entire game, eat with it on, and know that you know you're gonna be the one who is going to catch a foul ball! Side note, I've watched with a smile as kids have done this.

THIRD INNING: FIRSTS

They have even learned how to put a hot dog into a baseball glove while eating it. Don't even try to tell them to take it off because they know that at any moment a foul ball is coming their direction and they HAVE to be ready to catch it. Don't try to reason with them how they will be able to catch a ball with a giant hot dog in their baseball glove. They will look at you with disbelief, knowing that you don't have a foul ball in your life because you took your glove off to eat a hot dog, cotton candy, or some dumb peanuts. "Geez dude, don't you know anything about baseball?"

Those who calculate odds will tell you that it is a one in a 38,000 chance that you will ever catch a baseball at a Cubs game. But then again, those egg-headed math guys don't live with the kind of hope that exists among 120 kids with sweaty, stinky hands stuck in really small baseball gloves.

First Time Going to a Game with Dad

Another first for me was going to a Cubs game with my dad. He took me to a game. Not sure who else went with us, who we played, or much of anything else. I just knew my dad was sitting next to me and we were both cheering for the Cubs. He was so cool as he got us both a drink and a hot dog. This wasn't exactly a true Herculean task, but you would have had a hard time convincing me about that. I do remember the Cubs lost, but it didn't bother me at all. I got to sit next to my dad and that mattered even more than the game itself. Me and my dad were Cubs fans!

First Cubs Jersey

When you are a fan, you wear a lot of Cubs shirts. You'll even wear the lame ones your mom makes from a press on decal. At some point you will be a Cu fan or an ubs fan if your mom made you a shirt like that. But the day will come when you have your first, real Cubs jersey! What is weird is that I don't remember whose name was on my first Jersey. I know I currently have a Rizzo jersey. For me, it would have been fine if it was an Ernie Banks, or a Ron Santo, or a Billy Williams jersey. They were all my heroes. As a kid you even think that there is a remote possibility that if you wear it to a game they might mistake you for an actual Cubs player – and you'll get to play that day!

The wonder and imagination of a little kid at Wrigley delights my heart. Sure, I was delusional thinking that anyone would see me in my Ernie Banks jersey and think the following. "Hey, that little, 4 foot, white kid, whose head looks like a toe, that's Ernie Banks. Hey Ernie, get in here – you got a game to play!"

First True Souvenir

There are shirts and there are jerseys, but there is nothing like your very first Cubs souvenir. When I was a kid I mowed lawns to make money. One year I took a lot of that money to a Cubs game I attended. As I watched the game, ate a hot dog, drank a Coke, and ate peanuts I remembered a Cubs souvenir stand where I saw it! A baseball with genuine fake signatures of the previous years' Cubs lineup. I had to have it. I squirmed in my seat for most of that game hoping against hope that it would still be there after the game. Little did I know that they had about 100 of them in a box in the back. Each with the genuine fake signatures of the Cubs. It didn't matter to me. I bought it and treasured it until I went to college. Not sure what happened to it. That ball along with my genuine Ernie Banks jersey I wore when I was 8 could have brought me a fortune.

THIRD INNING: FIRSTS

My First of Many Cubs Loses

In addition to all these firsts was my first Cubs loss. Pretty sure that it didn't devastate me as I left the stadium with my stinky little hand still in my glove. (You never know when an after game foul ball may come your way!) I probably just wanted to get home and take off my Air-barfs from that kid who threw up on my row. Losing is something that a true Cubs fan deals with in life. The experience of seeing the Cubs live at Wrigley is worth it – win or lose. If you know true fandom you understand this. Your team is your team! Seeing them as they leave the dugout and run onto the field does something to you. When you learn to love a team as a child, loyalty is a given. You have your heroes. You have the field where they play etched into your mind. This is "your" team. You'll stick with them your whole life.

This was how it was before the modern age turned professional sports into a win or else thing. You wanted to pass the love of your team to your kids – and then watch them do the same with their kids. If you're lucky, you might even get to go to a game with 3 or 4 generations together. Wins are good – but they pale in light of how a family can enjoy being fans together. Sure, the Cubs lost all those games that I attended live. But honestly, I can't remember a single score from those early years. What I do remember is sitting with my buddies and sitting with my dad. Lose? Nah – those were wins – all of them.

Fourth Inning: Park District Mayhem

We only go to Cubs games

A baseballography needs scenes where a group of kids go to a game together. For me that was the Park District games. Straight out of "Rookie of the Year" or "The Sandlot." I was at a Cubs game with my buddies. Nothing compares to sharing a Cubs game with 120 of your buds who are all wearing baseball gloves. Since the Park District only went to Cubs games, that meant we pretty much were all a bunch of pint-sized Cubs fans, at least for a day.

120 kids – 4 adults – What could go wrong?

During the summer the Park District would go to a Cubs game. That's not all that hard to believe. What is hard to believe is that we filled two or three yellow buses with kids – and had 4-6 adults responsible for making sure they went to a major city and came home safe. I mean, what could go wrong? It was a different time.

We'd cram into those buses – 120 kids – 120 baseball gloves – and 120 bundles of energy and excitement ready to explode. Even though that sounds insane, I have to say that these trips went pretty smoothly. I don't remember any of us being on the side of a milk carton. To all those adults who took these trips with us – thank you!

Me and my buddies – Didn't know the organ could be so cool!

I am not an organ music fan. I never had an album of rock and roll's most famous church organ players. Yet, as I sat and watched multiple Cubs games, I was strangely amazed by how an organ player could move a crowd of thousands! He knew just want to play to get us to yell, "Charge!" at the perfect moment. We'd start clapping with him when he'd play a certain tune – probably called, "The Baseball Clapping Song." Throughout the game I never thought that this organ stuff was weird or square. (Sorry, had to use the language of the times for that comment.)

My buddies were all yelling and clapping with the organ dude as well. We never actually said it out loud, but the general thought was that we didn't know an organ player could be so cool! I know that today each player has special music for when they walk up to the plate, but I hope they never lose those really cool organ people. Baseball wouldn't be the same without them.

120 kids with baseball gloves – all disappointed

I know I wrote about this earlier, but I do remember seeing an entire section of little kids with baseball gloves on their hands. We were certain that we'd be catching a ball at the game. But the trip home always involved 120 kids all disappointed that they didn't catch a ball. Despite this being the case, 120 kids would once again show up next time, all with baseball gloves on their hands.

$5 to live it up

For some reason I remember getting a 5 dollar bill from my parents. Five dollars was a fortune to me. Sure, some rich kid would always show us the 20 his parents gave him, but it didn't matter. I could live it up for the day with my five bucks. That was enough for my hot dog, Coke, peanuts and a genuine Cubs score card (complete with tiny pencil!). Me and Abe Lincoln were going to party hardy for nine innings.

Buying a Genuine Cubs Scorecard (tiny pencil included)

One thing I have wondered about for years is why I ever bought a score card. We all did it. Somewhere in the recesses of our 6-8 year old minds we were sure that if you didn't have an Genuine Cubs Scorecard (tiny pencil included) you wouldn't be able to prove you were at the game.

I remember opening the card up and seeing all the boxes. There was a

FOURTH INNING: PARK DISTRICT MAYHEM

place available for you to keep up with the score of both teams. When I think about it, I probably couldn't write out their names – let alone know the Newtonian calculus needed to fill the thing out. There was always that one nerdy kid who would say, "it's easy, guys!" He'd dutifully fill out the required baseball hieroglyphics in all the right spots. At the end of the game, we'd look at his program with wonder and amazement. Thank goodness there was a spot that said "final score," or we wouldn't know who won the game. Well, unless we looked at the giant scoreboard with the score on it. Math is so hard at 6.

7th Inning Stretch

One of my favorite moments of any Cubs game is the seventh inning stretch. It was so cool to watch an entire stadium of people rise to their feet and sing, "Take Me Out to the Ball Game". I've heard it sung by Harry Carrey himself and several others. I had the honor of being at the Cubs game when Ernie Banks sang it for the last time before he passed away.

The words for this song are altered when sung at Wrigley. We do not sing, "Let me root, root, root for the home team," but use the proper words, "Root, root, root for the Cubbies." For some reason I always get hungry for Cracker Jack after singing that song.

As an adult I have learned a second song at Wrigley Field. It is only sung after a Cubs win. It is that dreaded song, "Go, Cubs Go." For anyone other than a Cubs fan, that may be the most hated song in all of baseball. But for those who are true Cubbies fans, it is music to our ears.

Park District game losses

LOVABLE LOSER

Every single game I attended with the illustrious Park District T-ball group ended up being a Cubs loss. Figuring that I went about twice a year for three years – the Cubs went 0-6 when I was there. Losing games was a consistent thing for me when I went to Wrigley Field. Yet, never once did I ever consider being anything but a Chicago Cubs fan.

Fifth Inning: Grown Up Cubs Fan

LOVABLE LOSER

FIFTH INNING: GROWN UP CUBS FAN

More Games with Dad

Getting older meant leaving behind the Park District T-ball days and slowly but surely becoming a grown up Cubs fan. I have to admit that I miss those days. They were innocent and fun. Everything around me seemed bigger than life when I was at Wrigley.

Getting older also meant going to games with my dad. He was not a perfect man, but he was larger than life to me. He was a tall man and pretty quiet for the most part. But the mystery seemed to make me want to be around him even more. Gone were the days when his gigantic hand would hold mine as we walked up to the iconic Wrigley entrance. Now we walked up together more as friends who wanted to see a Cubs game.

We didn't constantly attend games, just occasionally. That actually made it even more special. I was truly blessed to have a dad that was interested in me and interested in making a few memories with his son. I can't remember one time where it wasn't both fun and special

We are NOT sitting in the Bleachers!

As a fan, you dream of catching a home run hit by one of your baseball heroes. My guess is that this is the case no matter who you cheer for in Major League baseball. This posed a problem for me. There are only two ways of catching a home run when you are a Cubs fan. One involved standing outside the stadium and hoping that someone hits one out onto Waverly Avenue. That was not going to happen for me. When I went to a game - I was inside the stadium. So that meant there was only one way for me - sitting in the bleachers at Wrigley Field.

I remember begging my dad to buy us seats in the bleachers. There I could be the lucky guy who caught a homer hit by Ernie, or Billy, or Ron! But I knew the answer that was coming regardless of what face I tried to use on my dad. He'd look at me and say sternly, "We are NOT sitting in the bleachers!" There was no need to argue, hold my breath, or throw a fit. This conversation was finished. Weird thing is I never actually asked my dad why we couldn't sit in the bleachers.

For years I had all kinds of weird thoughts about this run through my head. Evidently only convicted felons, mass murderers, and surly mean-looking types were able to get tickets in the bleachers. Maybe they only gave tickets to people who were in the mob! As a kid I had visions in my head of Al Capone sitting there with 20 of his henchmen. Maybe they only allowed clowns to sit in the bleachers. If that were the case, I didn't need convincing. Clowns scared me spit-less. I guess some mysteries in life were never to be solved.

Sometimes when watching a game on WGN I'd see the people in the bleachers. Somebody would hit a homerun and there they were! Strangely they looked pretty much like everyone else I'd seen at games. Rather than question my dad's wisdom, I'd think, "That's what they want you to think. You're just sitting at a game in the bleachers, thinking you're having a great time - and then BOOM - it happens. You've been pulled into the mob, or you suddenly want to become a clown or even worse, a Cardinals fan!" Nope, not worth risking something like that happening!

Having a Genuine Cubs Scorecard (tiny pencil included) - With Dad Teaching me how to Fill it Out!

As I grew older, I began to learn higher levels of math. There was

FIFTH INNING: GROWN UP CUBS FAN

Algebra, Calculus, Trigonometry, and . . . how to fill out the Genuine Cubs Scorecard (tiny pencil included)! That was stepping way beyond even Einstein and the other guys who replaced numbers with letters! (I always felt like I left a part of my soul behind when I agreed to learn math in this way.)

This quantum leap in mathematical ability came because I had a true genius as my teacher - my dad! We'd get two Genuine Cubs Scorecards (tiny pencil included) and find our seats. The moment they would post the lineups on the big board, my genius dad would spring into action! He'd write the names of all the players into the space provided. Now that I was a little more literate - I sat there in rapt attention and would write down exactly what my dad was writing, in the exact spaces he was writing them. As the game progressed, my dad would alternate clapping and cheering with sitting down and writing what just happened in his scorecard. If I ever got confused, he'd show me how to write 6-3 or S for single - or whatever else had just happened. It was like I had learned a secret code!

When the game was over, he would help me count up all the hits, runs, and errors - and then with a sense of accomplishment only matched by other Rhodes scholars and Nobel prize winners - I'd have a completed Genuine Cubs Scorecard (tiny pencil dutifully used)! It only took a genius I got to call dad to move me into the world of baseball statistician status.

Still haven't caught a Dang Foul Ball

Time progressed and I went from pre-teen into my teen years. It didn't matter what time of life it was, I always enjoyed going to a Cubs game. I'm over 60 now and I still get goose bumps when I see Wrigley Field as I walk toward the stadium. They serve different food now and the area around Wrigley has definitely changed. Gone are the days when we'd drive around the neighborhood and pay for parking in someone's front yard. The heroes that I loved are gone - most of them enshrined in metal statues that are around the park. But the sheer joy of watching the Cubs is still there.

One thing has not changed though. I still haven't caught a dang foul ball. What is a little weird though, is that whenever one comes within a good 60 yards of where I am in the stands - I still have that moment where I'm sure that I'll be the guy that will catch it. If I did, I'd probably give it to a little kid who was sitting nearby - stinky hand stuck in his little baseball glove (filled with a full sized hot dog with mustard and ketchup on it - the glove, his hand, and his face). Nowadays I'd love to catch a foul ball just to see that little kid's eyes brighten as I give him a "real" baseball from a "real" Cubs game.

More Cubs Loses with Dad

Not exactly sure how many games I went to with my dad., but one thing didn't change. The Cubs lost all of them we attended live. One would think that I'd get frustrated with all this losing. Nah. I mean, I'm a Cubs fan - a true, blue Cubs fan. Losing was something we understood. We still loved our Cubbies.

Something about This Matters

I'll never regret any of those moments spent with my dad at a Cubs game. We even went to a Braves game together when we were in Atlanta one vacation. It is a legacy that I want to pass down to my sons. Something about this matters. It's not about the seats, or the real Genuine Cubs

FIFTH INNING: GROWN UP CUBS FAN

Scorecard (tiny pencil included). It's not about getting a hot dog and a Coke or even living with the eternal hope that you WILL catch a foul ball. it's way more important than that.

Throughout my life I've had good times and bad times. I've had moments of joy and moments of heartbreak. But there was just something truly special about going to a game with my dad. Something centering - something meaningful - something wonderful. Going to a game won't solve our world's problems - it won't cause world peace - it won't heal the sick or raise the dead. But it will cause a young boy - and even an older one to have memories that will never fade away. All you need to do is see a baseball field, hear the sound of a ball hitting a glove, or hear the sound of a wooden bat hitting a ball. Those things trigger a smile on my face. I'll remember sitting next to my real hero. I'll remember that really big man holding my hand as we crossed the street. I'll remember the dire warnings about the bleachers. I'll remember a grown man leaning over to help me fill out my scorecard (tiny pencil in a tiny hand included). If you've experienced it, you'll join me in saying, "Something about this matters."

Sixth Inning: Helping Your Kids Become Cubs Fans (OK Indoctrinating Them)

W**atching Games in Chicago on summer visits**

When my children were growing up, we'd travel to see the family in the Chicago area. We were the only ones who moved from the area, so we'd pack up whatever large volume vehicle we had at the time (I've got 6 kids) and we would take off for that town of thrill and excitement, Lockport, Illinois.

One of the highlights on these visits, and the ones around either Thanksgiving or Christmas, was being able to see Chicago games. That was a treat for me and for my kids, whom I was grooming to be Cubs and Bulls fans. We'd all cram into the family room and watch a baseball game or a basketball game together. There would be either popcorn or pizza as well as cheering for the Cubs.

Grandma Watches Games with us!

One of the great moments for me was watching my boys sit next to my mom to watch games. She was more of a Bulls fan than Cubs fan, but my boys absolutely loved it. The really loved it when mom would get worked up about the refs or a call that went against Chicago.

I remember my youngest son saying how cool it was to watch the games with Grandma. She only had boys and so, even though I had four girls, she would always make time in between cooking and playing games with the kids (she would regularly cheat at Boggle) to watch the game with the boys. I don't think I ever saw the boys leave a game to go do something else when their grandma was with them on the couch. She really disliked the Mets and the Knicks, so it was a real treat to watch with her when they played. Occasionally mom would let a less than lady like word slip out – especially if Patrick Ewing was playing. Having a mom who watched games with your kids really helped in getting them to be Cubs fans.

Won't buy them Contraband from other teams

One of the things you have to do when seeking to indoctrinate your kids into loving the Cubs is to clearly identify what is contraband. In my case it was the presence of any other baseball team's gear in the home. Between me and their grandma that was not difficult. It was a common thing for the boys to get Chicago paraphernalia as gifts at Christmas and on their birthday. It also didn't hurt on the rare occasion that we could attend a game while in the Chicago area.

Marriage and Changing Loyalty

When my daughters began to find their husbands, there was a cold wind that blew through our lives. Not the guys themselves – I liked them. But a couple daughters married locally. That meant that they married Cardinals fans. In fact, one of the weddings had a Cardinals' groom cake. I didn't eat any of it.

One of the funnier moments was when the Cubs were going to play against St. Louis in the playoffs. My son-in-law's family knew of our family curse (that the Cubs had never won when I was physically at a game). Let's just say that I was offered free tickets, transportation, and even my own hotel room in St. Louis when the games were there. Even though this was couched in a joking manner, I'm pretty sure if I had agreed to do this – it would have happened. My response though was to let them know that I was not planning on being within 100 miles of any venue where the Cubs played in a playoff game. I'm pretty sure that I would have turned down World Series tickets when they won, because I believed that if I was physically in the stadium, they would lose.

Like Father, Like Sons

My boys never faltered. They both followed in their dad's footsteps and became Cubs fans. We watched games together, even attending live if we could. We'd have the occasional discussion about the Cubbies and how they were doing. They are even encouraging their kids to cheer for the Cubs. My guess is that they are not quite as far gone in this matter as I am. Nevertheless, it doesn't hurt to help the next generation of Cubbies fans.

Our last game with Dad

I hate remembering the conversation with my mom. It was the day that it was confirmed that my dad had Alzhiemer's Disease. We saw that dad's memory wasn't like it was when he was younger – but we just all thought it was the aging process. The day came when we found out - Dad had Alzhiemer's. My heart sank and my eyes welled up with tears. Some people lose their dad all at once from a heart attack, but I lost mine slowly to a horrible disease.

A few days later I had one of the crazier conversations with my wife. Before my dad lost more of his memory, I wanted to take the boys with me to see one last Cubs game with my dad. Being the sweet, wonderful woman she is, she said yes and encouraged me to go to Chicago.

The trip to Chicago with the boys was a blast. We drove there while eating terrible fast food, telling horrible dad jokes, and just being three guys in a car on a road trip. I will always treasure those hours with my boys. We were on a mission to see the Cubs with my dad. It was something I wanted to do – no, in a way, I had to do. I wanted them to have one last memory with me – and with their grandfather. It was one of the things I loved doing with him. Maybe I just wanted them to be able to say they had that same memory too.

We arrived and the next day and shortly afterward, had the tickets to the Arizona Diamondbacks game. It was a day game – so we got to watch the Cubs old style. That day I did all the things we normally did at Wrigley Field. We bought hot dogs and drinks, we bought a Genuine Cubs Scorecard (tiny pencil included). We did all the things I did as a kid with my dad (minus the stinky hand stuck in the little baseball glove). We watched the game – hoped the Cubs would win – were disappointed when they didn't – and then drove home together bubbling with stories and things to say to each other.

Baseball did that for me and my dad. There were other times when we would struggle to talk – but a day with the Cubs seemed to loosen all those awkward barriers and conversation would flow. It was as if for a day, Alzhiemers didn't matter and my dad could think and talk with us like old times. I won't ever forget that day. Don't think my sons will either. We were with dad and grandad, we were watching the Cubs, and we were truly enjoying time with each other. Like I said earlier, something about this mattered.

Seventh Inning: 36 in a Row!

A Strange Set of Circumstances

I'm not really sure when this dawned on me. I know that I was an adult when it happened. As I reminisced about being a Cubs fan, I began to remember all the games that I had attended. It was kind of like scrolling through photographs in my mind. As I looked at each picture, a memory would come to me.

It was fun to start counting up the games that I had been to over the years. Each picture initiated a wonderful set of memories. There were the Park District games, the games with my dad, games with buddies, and games with my kids. There wasn't a single one I didn't like. Then it hit me.

Hey – I've never seen the Cubs win a game "live"

Suddenly it hit me that I had never seen the Cubs win a game "live". Every time I went into Wrigley or any other stadium, the Cubs lost! How could this be? At the time I had been to around 30-35 different games in person and never once did the score board announce to me that my favorite team had won!

Slowly a thought began to invade my mind. It's not just that the Cubs have a curse when it comes to winning the World Series, I have a personal curse that prevents the Cubs from winning whenever I step into the place they're playing! To most this will sound like I need help, and maybe I did (or still do). But to a true, blue Cubs fan, this would make perfect sense.

As fans, Cubs supporters have lived lives that seem to defy reason. It took over 100 years for us to win a World Series. We collapsed in 1969 and the Mets won the pennant when we lost 17 of 25 games in September. We had the Steve Bartman incident in 2003 that propelled the Florida Marlins to the World Series. We refused to let a goat come to a game and have been cursed by said goat-ghost ever since! And now – we've got a guy as a fan who makes us lose every stinking time he enters the stadium! It all made sense. At least it made sense to a guy from Lockport, who now lived in Arkansas, and, who evidently had way too much time on his hands.

Cubs vs. Expos (sure thing gone wrong)

Immediately, I began to plan how to break this curse. One summer my boys and I were offered free tickets to see the Cubs at Wrigley. When I looked at the date and the team we were going to be playing, it was the Expos. My heart jumped when I saw that. The Expos sucked! This would be the perfect game to break the curse!

We arrived at the game convinced that this was the day! We did all the usual things – hot dog, drink, Genuine Cubs Scorecard (tiny pencil included), and we sat in amazing seats, behind third base. We watched the game as it progressed and soon began to doubt when the Cubs fell behind by 2. Then it began to happen right in front of our eyes!

It was the ninth inning and we were down by two. Our hearts leaped or sank with every batter. But something more important was going on that many were unaware of that day. It began as the inning started and all three of us looked at each other and said, "Rally hats!" We proceeded to take off our Cubs hats, turn them inside out, and put them on backwards. We could see it in each other's eyes, that should do it.

Then came the first out. We looked at each other in a panic – and immediately took off our Cubs shirts and turned them inside out – then put them back on again. Once again, we turned to each other and saw it clearly – there, that should guarantee a win. Then came a hit, and another! Two guys were on base and the curse was going to go down in flames!

Second out. Suddenly we became frantic. We took off our shoes and socks. Turned the socks inside out and put them back on – then we turned our shoes backwards and tried as best we could to wear them backwards. I can only imagine at this point some of those watching this strange ritual considered calling for security. Instead, they followed our lead. All around us rally hats were on everyone's head. That may have been enough for them, but we were desperate. We all took off our belts and turned them around backwards – then we took off our watches and put them on backwards (by the way, that is really hard to do). We were undeterred by any level of difficulty before us.

Then we saw it – and nearly lost it. Sammy Sosa walked up to the plate. Turning to each other we blurted out in unison – homer! But it wasn't just going to be any homer – it was going to be a walk-off home run! Our family curse was going to be broken by a walk-off home run by Sammy Sosa! This was just too good to be true!

I don't remember how many pitches were in Sammy's at bat. I'd love to tell you it was 3 and 2, but I just don't remember. I just remember the sound of his bat hitting the ball. I had heard that sound before. It was the sound of a home run being hit. Here we go!

It was one of those moments when you know the crowd was roaring – but when we all heard "that" sound, everything got quiet. So many people were sucking in air with their mouths open that I think the entire north side of Chicago was without oxygen for 10 seconds. We watched as the outfielder went back and back. He went onto the warning track and suddenly jumped into the air as he hit the storied ivy-covered wall in left field. Then – then . . .

He caught the ball as he hit the wall. He held onto it as he came off the wall. He caught the dad-gum ball. In a moment, silence turned to people uttering a groan of disappointment as the third out was recorded and the Cubs lost to the Expos that day.

The three of us stood their looking like inside out weirdos. We groaned too - and then broke out into uncontrollable laughter. I don't know if we lost our minds for a moment, or we just had a very strange as inevitability set in. We saw how ridiculous we looked and just lost it laughing. Rather than curse the darkness of the moment – our strange sense of humor found this inevitability very, very funny.

We were sad our Cubbies had lost. But on the drive home we were our usual talk-crazy selves. We continued to laugh and enjoy each other. We even postulated together as to how we may have caused this. Did we sit in the wrong order? Did we buy the wrong food? Did we actually need someone to have a stinky hand in a ball glove for the entire day? We didn't know in the end, but we knew one thing. We loved being there with each other – and once again – it would be a day we would never forget.

Minor Leagues – Stacking the Deck

After this event, I was convinced I needed a new tack in my journey to my first live win with the Cubs. So, I did what any red-blooded, guilt-ridden, curse-carrying man would do. I cheated.

We lived in Jonesboro, Arkansas at the time, and that meant that the Memphis Redbirds team was about an hour away. They were a St. Louis Cardinals affiliate. But more important to us, they played the Iowa Cubs multiple times every year. My job involved planning events occasionally so that a group could enjoy a day together. So, I decided to have us go to a Redbirds game. Since I got to choose the date – I chose the game against the Iowa Cubs. Yes, I see you've figured out my ruse here. I could break the curse by seeing the Cubs win a minor league game!

Not so fast, buddy!

The fateful day arrived as we drove to Memphis, parked with the group, and headed for AutoZone Park, home of the Memphis Redbirds. That day I had three extra tickets. For someone as cheap as I am – that meant I could possibly sell them and get something better to eat at the game. So as the game started, I was outside trying to do my best impression of a scalper. I stink at impressions. When I realized that I had missed the entire first inning, I quickly accosted three boys walking together and asked them if they wanted to see the game. They were thrilled as I gave them the tickets and I broke into an old-guy run for the stadium. (An old-guy run doesn't really look like running. It might pass for someone being lazy while trying to walk briskly. It actually looks like an old guy trying to hurry – but being very bad at it).

As I entered the Stadium, I quickly found my seats and my very excited son. He quickly informed me of what had happened in the first inning. "Dad, it was incredible! We're knocking the cover off the ball! We scored 4 runs in the first inning. Then our pitcher struck out the side on 10 pitches! Today is the day, dad! We're going to win and break the curse!"

I looked up at the scoreboard and saw that it was 4-0 at the top of the second inning. This was the day. But I should have remembered. I wasn't in the stadium for that entire first inning. I only entered after the inning was over.

Not so fast, buddy! What took place after that was truly astounding. To say that the Iowa Cubs fell apart would be an understatement. Later in the 8th inning, with the score Memphis 9, Cubs 4, my son turned to me in shock and horror. He laughed as he made the statement, "Dad, I love you, but please leave the stadium." It was true. Since the moment my size 11 ½ shoe stepped over the entrance, the Cubs went from being a sure winner to losers. At that moment I had to face the facts. It wasn't a family curse – I was the reason the Cubs had lost all these games.

Revisiting the Bleachers

Fast forward to the day I rebelled against my dad. It was that opening day game I went to where Ernie Banks sang for the seventh inning stretch. If you haven't already figured it out yet, I had bought tickets in the bleachers. I was by myself, but was sitting next to a very nice couple as we braved the cold of an early season game in Chicago. If they knew the identity of who they sat next to, they probably would have thrown me over the wall onto Waverly Avenue.

The Cubs lost that day – duh. I watched as we fell behind and were unable to score in the final 3 innings. I knew it was because of me – but I didn't want to let anyone know. I mean, I was in the bleachers, and of all the areas that were dangerous for me to be – the bleachers were the worst!

On a side note, I understood by the end of the game why my dad said he wouldn't get tickets for the bleachers. It was the wildest game I had ever seen. People were throwing beers on each other for little or no reason. I saw a guy urinate in his beer cup in the stands one inning. During the seventh inning stretch I watched another guy run down the steps to the outfield wall – pull a urn from under his coat – and dump what I figured were his father's ashes through the basket and onto the centerfield warning track. Late in the ninth inning two groups in different sections began screaming at each other, itching for a fight. They blamed each other for the Cubs loss that day (I knew better). That situation calmed down when the leader of one group yelled at the leader of the other group. This man had removed his shirt revealing a beer belly that even Ron Santo couldn't match. His nemesis in the other section yelled at him, "Hey man, you're really fat!" The chubby fan agreed loudly. The fight was over. They all returned to the task of finishing their last beer. The great bleacher brawl of 2018 was averted. Needless to say, when I went to future games, I never bought bleacher seats again. (Oh, I also turned down offers to join the mob and become a clown – listen to your dad!)

Eighth Inning: The Magic Year!

LOVABLE LOSER

Watching the Cubs on MLB.com

Getting older meant being able to watch the Cubs on a

EIGHTH INNING: THE MAGIC YEAR!

regular basis. Major League Baseball had come out with MLB.com and I could buy a year's worth of Cubs games to watch. Now I could watch and be a part of more games without having to bring the curse into the stadium. Evidently the curse was not airborne.

This meant that in 2016 I could watch a lot of Cub wins. We started winning game regularly. This did not escape my notice of me or my sons. We were pretty excited that the Cubs were doing so well. Anthony Rizzo, Chris Bryant, Ben Zobrist, Jon Lester, Willson Contreras, Dexter Fowler, Jason Heyward, Grampa Rossy, these were names that became etched into my memory.

Is This Crazy Talk?

Could we actually win a World Series? That seemed like crazy talk to us as we talked that year. Maybe we'll make it to the World Series? As time went on, it became clear that this was going to happen!

I'll have to admit it. There were times when I was like a pitcher who had a no-hitter on the line. Don't say anything to anyone. Don't even talk about a NL Central crown – or a NL pennant. If you say something, it'll jinx it. Then came the win that put us in the World Series. The thought that this was crazy was over. The Cubs were in the World Series!

Should I Watch or Not – Revisiting the Airborne Theory

The first game of the World Series was that night. It was then that I decided to revisit the "airborne theory" of baseball curses. Could someone actually affect a game by watching it on TV. Not sure I spent that much time on this – but I came to the conclusion that previous data proved I could watch games – even playoff games - without causing problems for the Cubs. So, I began to watch.

It was pretty crazy watching that seven game series. My sons both lived in different cities so we couldn't watch them together. But that didn't keep us from texting each other about them. We were getting more and more excited every game. Then came Wednesday's final game.

At this point I should tell you I am a pastor of a church. I have responsibilities on Wednesday nights at our mid-week service. God had been dealing with me about my Cubs issues. I realized that I needed to choose God and my responsibilities that Wednesday night. So, I taught at church and made myself available to people afterward. Because I knew that people were going to be blowing up my phone with texts about the game – I turned it off.

When the evening was finished, I went to my office to close up and turned my phone on. My phone immediately blew up with about 50-60 texts.

Dad, Where are You? I'm Jumping up and Down on my Couch!

I realized that everyone was asking me how I was doing during the game. But then I read my son's texts. They were normal at first – but by around 8:10 p.m. they began to get frantic. I wasn't answering. So that meant that either I had been abducted by aliens who hated baseball, or, I was dead! Why else would dad not answer texts during game 7 of the World Series!

I quickly texted both sons and assured them I was OK. As I arrived home and turned on the game, I suddenly got very excited at what was happening right before my eyes. I quickly caught up with everything that had happened. My youngest son texted me that he was jumping up and down on his couch he was so excited.

Like every other Cubs fan, that night seemed like a dream, then a nightmare, then a perfect ending. We watched as we had the lead, then lost it to a home run. We watched as the game had a rain delay. It didn't matter to us if the game restarted at 3 in the morning – we were not going to miss this! Then we watched as we once again regained the lead with Ben Zobrist's double in the 11th inning. But nothing topped when Chris Bryant fielded that last out at third base and threw it to Anthony Rizzo at first. Cubs win! Cubs win the World Series!

The curse was broken. I talked with both sons that night. Not sure if I slept much. I was not usually a postgame guy, but that night I watched every moment of every postgame show. Most people won't understand this, but we had the longest futility streak of any team in modern sports. Now it was over. Most of us just sat and wondered if we could believe what we just saw. The only other thing I remember thinking that night was a wish that I could have seen it with my dad. It would have been wonderful to see him add up all the hits, runs, and errors on his Genuine Cubs Scorecard (tiny pencil included). At the end it would have read in the simplest terms, Cubs 8, Indians 7.

Ninth Inning: The Curse Breaker

36 Games Live – Without a Single Win

For most Cubs fans this book would have ended with the 2016 World Series win. But this is not about the lovable losers – it is about this lovable loser. I had added up all the games and come to the conclusion that I was 0-36 when watching the Cubs live. That particular curse had yet to be broken.

What had started as a family curse – had proven to be far more personal. Our family had a goat – and I was him. I didn't live from day to day carrying this around as some kind of horrible burden. It was more like a family joke. It was something I shared with other baseball fans who would laugh with me. Wow 0-36, that's weird.

A Time of Sadness – No Dad, No Mother, No Older Brother

I'm the youngest of three brothers. That meant that as we got older, I was most likely to be around when the rest of the family died. My dad died of Alzhiemers, and my mom died of complications from a stroke. I was left to watch over my oldest brother who was disabled. He wanted to stay in Lockport, so that meant I would visit him 2 to 3 times a year

NINTH INNING: THE CURSE BREAKER

to check on him. Then, he died suddenly of natural causes. That meant that I would have to make arrangements for his burial.

My sweet wife and I took a week to do all this. We travelled to Lockport and closed out my brother's financial life and prepared for a sad yard sale where we would sell what was left of his life. One day when things were winding down, I asked Sherie if she wanted to go see a Cubs game with me. She had never gotten to go to a game because she was faithfully holding down the fort with our four girls. We bought tickets and drove up to Chicago to see the Cubs play the St. Louis Cardinals.

No Curse?

As we walked up to Wrigley that night, I had no idea what was about to happen, but it was another night I will never forget. It was the night that my personal curse of 0-36 was broken. We found our seats and I prepared myself for the usual experience when I attended a game in person - another loss. But tonight was different. I watched as my beloved Cubbies got and kept the lead all the way down to the last out. With both shock and surprise I looked up at the scoreboard and it read, Cubs 7, Cardinals 6.

When the game was over, I kissed my wife and texted my kids. We even took a picture of the event that is now famous to my kids and friends. In it, my wife is standing with both arms held high with the winning score just to her left. Little did I know that I had a personal curse breaker next to me all those years. Curse-breaker - that is the name my boys quickly gave their mom. They also informed me that unless their mom came along – they would no longer attend Cubs games live with me. Who would have known that this lovable loser was married to a lovable winner!

About a year later we decided to visit Chicago again. We enjoyed a few days going to see a show, visiting the museums, eating deep dish pizza, and you got it, going to another Cubs game. In her own wonderful way, my lovable winner kept her streak alive. The Cubs won and her record is now 2-0.

We've not been able to go to a Cubs game with the boys – but I'm certain that if we do, they will get to watch a win. They have to. They would be with the Curse-breaker. For me this was the best possible way to end my personal curse – with the most important person in my world at my side.

Post Game Interview

Writing this has made me think. There is one thing I want to say in my post-game interview. I want to encourage dads to do what my dad did. Take your kids to a game. It doesn't matter if its baseball, football, or even an exciting Curling match in Canada. Take them with you and enjoy time sitting with them.

Personally, I would choose baseball. The reason for this is that baseball has natural breaks in the game – 9 of them to be exact. Each one can be an opportunity to talk with your son – maybe even be his hero. Our kids, especially our sons need heroes like never before, I'm not referring to the ones on the field. I am referring to the one sitting next to them at the game.

Don't get so caught up in work and striving for financial and career success. There is a little guy (or girl) who needs you far more than your company. While at the game you can have nine times to be with your child. Who knows, you may even want to get a Genuine Scorecard (tiny pencil included) and teach your children how to score a game. Whatever you do, don't do it on a phone or tablet. Do it on that Scorecard. If you don't have one of those, you won't be able to prove you've been to a game. Oh, and there is one other thing. Teach your son or daughter how to wear a little baseball glove on their hand all the way to the game. Let them have the hope of catching that foul ball (even if they don't). Who knows, if you're lucky you might get to hold that little stinky hand on the way out of the stadium. You might even get to hold that little hand and have a boy (just like me) look up into their father's face and think, "That's my hero." Not a bad reward for loving and taking the time to raise a lovable loser.

You know, maybe this wasn't a baseball-ography.

Maybe it was a father-and-son-ograpahy?

Made in United States
Orlando, FL
25 June 2024